Threads of Grace
Selected Poems

MARY F. LENOX

To: Nancy
Blessings & Peace!
Love, Mary F. Lenox
6-27-17

First Printing, October 2015

ISBN 9780578167534

LCCN: 2015914118

Book Design: Lynn Winston / Powell Graphics & Communication

ACKNOWLEDGMENTS

Thanks to friends, family,
and Brown Bag Poets
of the Chicago Cultural Center
for constant and generous support

Author's Note

Poetry is seeing the sacred in the ordinary.
A poem might begin with a thought, a feeling, a touch,
a smell
A sound, an "a-ha" moment that ignites the imagination.
It's a grace moment. In life there are infinite threads
of grace.

> Threads of grace
> Everywhere
> Sights and sounds
> Here and there
> Trees, shrubs, waterfalls, too
> Echo day anew
> Stop
> Look
> You will see
> Gifts of diversity
> Awaiting your embrace
> Feel
> Spirit, time, and place
> There you will find
> Endless grace

Table of Contents

Life & Love

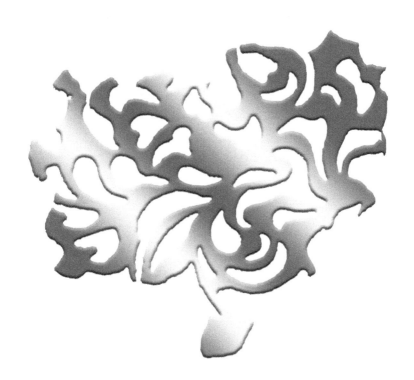

Ode to Love

The search for love
Begins from within
With full acceptance
Of all parts
Unconditionally
Completely
Wholly
Regardless
Then
You will receive
That which is there
Awaiting your embrace

Gift

Oh

How beautiful the day

When peace abides

Come what may

Oh

How beautiful this day

When peace abides

Come what may

Rhythm of Life

There are as many ways to dance

As there are people dancing

There are as many songs to sing

As there are singers

There are as many ways to love

As there are grains of sand on the shore

So just start where you are

And

Keep dancing, singing, and loving

What If

What is a song

If it is not sung

What is a dance

If it is not danced

What is a poem

If it is not spoken

 What is a book

If it is not read

What is life

If it is not lived

Endings

Life and death are partners

In the ebb and flow of changes

With the passing of a beloved

Grief can feel overwhelming

Yet

In time

Sadness will leave

Replaced by Spirit

That remains as an eternal flame

In heart, mind, and spirit

You've Got to Move

When Spirit

Gives utterance

Welcome energy of change

Align yourself with

Peace

Power

Love

Creativity

Passion

Live each moment

With gratitude

Shine in

Newness of life

Hold on to Hope

In the darkest night

Travel lightly

Into the unknown

With awakened faith

Let go of the temptation

To turn back or give up

Just keep walking

Step by step

Toward the Light

Ever present

Closeness

Come rest in the bosom of friendship

Linger there for a while

Rejoice in gifts of sharing

Encouragement with a smile

Smell the aroma of acceptance

Celebrate unconditional love

Feel the Spirit of kindness

Straight from the heart

Heavenly

Droplets

Gentle as a lover's touch

Infuse morning atmosphere

So like the tenderness

Of divine love

Always present

Gray skies

Or not

Moments

A Moment

Regal gray billows
Embrace mighty lake
With
 A loving hug
Of rain!

Morning Vibes

The downpour fell

Onto windows

Like miniature waterfalls

Slowly drifting downward

Toward a destination

Known only to the rain

Awakened Day

Dewdrops on roses
Make no sound
Unlike nearby waterfall
Yet
Both echo divine beauty
In the rhythm of this morn

Slowly Awakening

In early morn

Fog descends on skyscrapers

Reminiscent of Yosemite's Half Dome

None can escape

The murky haze of wetness

Surrounding

Earth and sky

Yet

Life continues

As we plow through it all

With the determination

Of a tortoise

I Wish

I want to get inside of you

To feel the texture of your spirit

Smell the fragrance of your incredible essence

And smile with joy!

Alas

Guess I'll have to sit on the shore

And watch surfers

Play in the sea

The Web

There it was
Waving in the wind
In foggy mist
Of a Monet like morning
Held in space
By uneven strands
Attached to nameless weeds
Fresh dewdrops
Clinging to its surface
Announcing the presence
Of this mysterious creation
Seeking to entice visitors
To the circle of
Hope and death

Amazing Grace

There he sat
As a finely chiseled bronze statue
So perfectly still
On top of a concrete pillar adjacent to the street
His spectacular body so shiny
With sculpted muscles
Born of intense efforts at the gym
Then he moved his bare chest
Ever so slightly
For a moment
Affirming that he was not an illusion
But a real living being
Incredible!

Early Morn

Blue surrenders to dense haze

Shimmering waters dance

In shades of gray

Break through of sparse light

Offers fresh hope

Now gone

In presence of spring rain

Contrasts

Dawn of light
Like cat eyes
Pierce through
Dense black clouds
Silence
Surrenders
To roar of motorists
Rushing to and fro
Darkness fades
Luminous glow
Struggles
To break through
Gloomy haze
Hope rises
In heart
Patiently waiting
For the sun
To smile

Seasons

Brrr!

One sunless afternoon
Winter arrived in Chicago
With mixture
Of dense fog and snowy rain
Such an abrupt rush of climate change
That takes your breath away
Time for boots and gloves
And all those wintry things   `
To protect us all
From chill, wind, and arctic cold
That will be with us
Till
Spring

Missouri Visitor

Then it came
The last snow of winter
Silently falling
Amid gentle winds
Landscape covered
In blanket of pure whiteness
Invites mind
To behold its beauty
Once more
Before the spring thaw

Mournful March

Night snow
Covers pier and park
Dense fog
Fills atmosphere
Fresh born spring
Invaded by wintry chill
Snow falls like rain
Then ceases
At midday
Lake surrenders
To it all
Awaiting the demise
Of winter

Summer Gift

It was so hard to say goodbye
To the last farm fresh strawberry of the season
Its tart flavor invites
Surrender to delicious sweetness
So few bites to savor
As it becomes a part of my body
Its essence transformed
Into newness of life
With only the memory to comfort my sadness
Now that it is gone
As it once was
This receptacle of nature
So plump, tender, and juicy
Just another reminder
To savor every moment
Before it becomes
Once upon a time

What Season?

Scattered clouds like giant cotton balls
Surround skyscrapers
Bitter cold
Intense
As hottest day of summer
Disregards calendar announcing
First day of spring
Wintry atmosphere
Chills to the bone
Like ice chips embedded in your long johns
Oh well
It's another Chicago day
That refuses to surrender

Mosquito Heaven

Walking in Indiana woods
She encountered
Countless mosquitoes
Flying freely
Amid dense trees
Their canopy
Left moisture
From recent rains
With July warmth of sun
Infusing morning air
They welcomed the visitor
With numerous bites
Of breakfast delight
Of bloody Mary
She couldn't escape them
Surrender
Became her only option
Finally
Finding refuge in her car
All the while
Birds chirping
Near and far

Fall Grace

Even as the leaves of pumpkin and gold tones

Embrace the landscape

This November morn

They offer their final gift of beauty

In their rich, deep hues of death

Commentary

The Great Migration

they came with hope and created possibilities
travelers
hundreds thousands countless more
one by one
making the decision
to leave the past for an unknown future
they came from
alabama, tennessee, mississippi, georgia,
north carolina, south carolina, florida
and so many other regions of the south
Looking to embrace new life in the " promised land"
of the north
they came to
detroit, chicago, new york, los angeles,
philadelphia, and MANY other cities and towns
mothers, fathers,sisters, brothers
they came
grandmothers, grandfathers, children, the yet unborn
they came
uncles, aunts, cousins, nieces,
nephews

they came
by train, car, walking
they came
from rural roots
to urban sprawl
they came
Some money, little money, no money
a sandwich
a name or two
of relatives and friends who had already made the
journey
they came
living in kitchenettes, apartments, church havens,
ghetto spaces beyond imagination
still
they came
no job, no education
Yet
they came
they
could not
would not
dare not
turn around

so

they held a prayer in their hearts

and faith that "the lord will make a way"

moment by moment

step by step

day by day

connecting to the divine

each other, and with the help of others,

created schools, churches, communities

businesses, music, literature, art

cultural expressions denied for 400 years

all the while

believing that they could and would build

new lives

from remnants of hope

AND SO

THEY DID!

Consequences

You knew you shouldn't have done it

But you did it anyway

So sad

You'll have to pay

Today or someday

Saturday Surprise

She was driving down Michigan Avenue
In soft mist
When suddenly
Amid decaying homes
 A spectacular garden
Adjacent to a glorious house
Came into view
This vision of glory
Saying
HERE I STAND
Beauty can be created
Regardless of lost dreams
Long gone in Chicago
HERE I STAND
Still showing what's achievable
With relentless courage
To create
In spite of surroundings
HERE I STAND
Demonstrating possibilities
While surviving poverty and hopelessness
HERE I STAND
Shining in the midst of chaos
Reflecting joyful promise
For all to see

Gettysburg: 150 Years Later

Life continues even at Gettysburg
150 years after the carnage
Of that great battle of the American Civil War
Birds, flowers, and trees did not participate
In the epic conflict of death
Of northern and southern soldiers
Fighting for union or separation of a nation
Now we know
In spite of all that occurred there
The natural world renews itself
Ever marching toward life
Regardless

The Day After

At almost sunset
In the distant western sky of Chicago
Gentle rain
Like ribbons of heavenly light
Falls softly from billowing clouds
As if crying for the bomb victims of the Boston
Marathon
Their joy so brutally stolen in an instant of insanity

On the day after the unthinkable tragedy
Vivid images of people
Shocked beyond words still fill the airwaves
Rushing toward the carnage
To assist the living and mourn the dead
While others fleeing the scene
Unable to find a safe haven to nurture their disbe-
lief

The sadness too broad and deep to process
The inconceivable and unbelievable
Still hurt so very much

Through it all
We continue
With fresh awareness of the precious
gift of life
And the need to give and receive love
Everyday

Baltimore Riot

Night of rage
Born
Not of yesterday
But for many moons
Festering community sores
Now ruptured
After a murderous incident with police
Another African American male
Dead in the streets
For what or why?
Fire
Fights
Violent destruction
Chaos
Fear
In darkness of anger
Daylight brings an uneasy calm
Healing hope
Not yet real
God help us all
For they know not what they do!

The Big Squeeze

Chilly rains
In late spring
Fill the atmosphere
Fog meets skyscrapers
In a shroud of dense haze
Raindrops weep
At the big squeeze
Eastward
Lakefront affluence
Westward
Oakbrook opulence
In between
Fourteen miles of vast wasteland
People struggling to make ends meet
In a sea of nail salons, beauty shops,
Fast food, boarded up promises
Churches, big and small,
Closed shut
Offer scant hope
This side of Jordan
God have mercy on us all
Does anybody know
Or care
About what's really going on?

Commentary   45

Wonderous Day

There they were

Two friends

Tall

Young

Handsome

Leaning against the brick wall

Sharing secrets

In the sun

Who will die first

Bit by bit

After smoking

Many cigarettes?

The Witness

Partially hidden from view
Three baby robins high up in a tree nest
Mama robin comes along with a wiggling worm
Its body soon pulled apart by the newborns
Papa flies in with another sacrificial lamb
To feed his hungry brood
Death and life seen
In afternoon drama
Parents then fly away
Separately
To continue the cycle
Nestlings
Unconscious of the process
That gives them life
Eagerly awaiting the next offerings
Of love
Mouths open
Heads high
Chirping in the wind
On a Sunday afternoon
In July

Time

The Gift of time

Is what it is

When you rush

You refuse to accept it

Thus

Leaving it waiting

For you!

Aging

What to do when dark clouds of change
Implode your sense of security
   Eyes dim
   Body aches
   Memory fades
Look for the light of grace
To awaken fresh hope
   Receive love
   Ever present
Here, there, and everywhere
   Live in Spirit
Regardless of passing circumstances

Remembrance

The sun did not forget to rise this dawn
Its radiant glow
Like clockwork
Ascends into blue skies
It did not forget
To anoint the atmosphere
With luminous light
It did not forget
To warm the spirit with fresh hope
 It did not forget
To kiss the sparse clouds with brightness
It remembered to do what it does everyday
Be light to the world
Why can't we be like the sun?

Mary F. Lenox

I write everyday

To smile with gratitude

As I feel, hear, taste, touch,

smell and see

The sacred in the ordinary

Secrets revealed

Amid

Earth and sky

Space and time

Observing

People, places, and things

Outside my window and elsewhere

I write everyday

To express

Word pictures

Imagined in new ways

I write everyday

To contemplate the notion of beauty

To perceive

With body, mind, spirit, and emotions

Then

To remember

Again and again

Moments of inspiration

I write everyday

With hope

That my poetry

May evoke:

A thought

A feeling

A curiosity

An appreciation

A joyful sound

Maybe

It will arouse

A wondrous instant

Worthy of remembrance

I write everyday

Because it gives fresh life

To every cell of my being

I write everyday

To honor the spirit of:

Inspiration

Imagination

Insight

Gratefulness

I write everyday

To discover and uncover

My innermost thoughts and feelings

While witnessing and experiencing life

As I come of age

Finally

CPSIA information can be obtained
at www.ICGtesting.com
Printed in the USA
LVOW05s1209090617

537473LV00017B/172/P